Wonderful God Wonderful Me

PUBLISHING & *Enterprises*

by Amy Kleman

Wonderful God, Wonderful Me
Copyright © 2008 by Amy Kleman. All rights reserved.

This title is also available as a Tate Out Loud product. Visit www.tatepublishing.com for more information.

No part of this publication may be reproduced, stored in a retrieval system or transmitted in any way by any means, electronic, mechanical, photocopy, recording or otherwise without the prior permission of the author except as provided by USA copyright law.

The opinions expressed by the author are not necessarily those of Tate Publishing, LLC.

Published by Tate Publishing & Enterprises, LLC
127 E. Trade Center Terrace | Mustang, Oklahoma 73064 USA
1.888.361.9473 | www.tatepublishing.com

Tate Publishing is committed to excellence in the publishing industry. The company reflects the philosophy established by the founders, based on Psalm 68:11,
"The Lord gave the word and great was the company of those who published it."

Book design copyright © 2008 by Tate Publishing, LLC. All rights reserved.
Cover design & Interior design by Eddie Russell
Illustration by Greg White

Published in the United States of America

ISBN: 978-1-60696-368-5
1. Youth & Children: Children: General
2. Juvenile Non Fiction: Religion: Inspirational
08.07.22

For

Brooke, Brady, Annabelle, and Andrew.

Mommy loves you.

God,
you know me better than anybody else.

Your ways are wonderful.

You see me always. Wherever I am, you are with me.

You
hold me in your hand.

You made me like you made the stars in the sky.

You
put me together and watched over me as I grew in my mother's womb.

The day I was born, **you** were there.

You
made me
special.

You know all the days of my life.

You are God.
are God.

LORD, you have examined me and know all about me. You know when I sit down and when I get up. You know my thoughts before I think them. You know where I go and where I lie down. You know everything I do. LORD, even before I say a word, you already know it. You are all around me—in front and in back—and have put your hand on me. Your knowledge is amazing to me; it is more than I can understand. Where can I go to get away from your Spirit? Where can I run from you? If I go up to the heavens, you are there. If I lie down in the grave, you are there. If I rise with the sun in the east and settle in the west beyond the sea, even there you would guide me. With your right hand you would hold me. I could say, "The darkness will hide me. Let the light around me turn into night."

But even the darkness is not dark to you. The night is as light as the day; darkness and light are the same to you. You made my whole being; you formed me in my mother's body. I praise you because you made me in an amazing and wonderful way. What you have done is wonderful. I know this very well. You saw my bones being formed as I took shape in my mother's body. When I was put together there, you saw my body as it was formed. All the days planned for me were written in your book before I was one day old. God, your thoughts are precious to me. They are so many! If I could count them, they would be more than all the grains of sand. When I wake up, I am still with you.

Psalm 139:1–18

listen|imagine|view|experience

AUDIO BOOK DOWNLOAD INCLUDED WITH THIS BOOK!

In your hands you hold a complete digital entertainment package. Besides purchasing the paper version of this book, this book includes a free download of the audio version of this book. Simply use the code listed below when visiting our website. Once downloaded to your computer, you can listen to the book through your computer's speakers, burn it to an audio CD or save the file to your portable music device (such as Apple's popular iPod) and listen on the go!

How to get your free audio book digital download:

1. Visit www.tatepublishing.com and click on the e LIVE logo on the home page.
2. Enter the following coupon code:
   1874-2b26-f04b-2bfa-e99d-46de-3800-fcec
3. Download the audio book from your e LIVE digital locker and begin enjoying your new digital entertainment package today!